'Til the Slipper Fits

Godly Encouragement for Single Women

Melissa Gayle

Contents

Foreword

I wrote the initial draft of this book in the summer of 2005. In December of 2006, my younger sister married her prince. I was her *maid* of honor. It was a thrill to be her honored attendant, but it was also one of the hardest things I have ever had to do. In fact, I couldn't think about the reality of the ceremony during the wedding or I would have bawled during the entire thing. But I had prayed for months beforehand that I would be able to make it through the ceremony, and God was very good and got me through.

I know what it's like to go through tough times as a single woman longing to no longer be alone. I have dealt with car trouble, physical problems, intense loneliness, job changes and difficulties, weddings, and even depression, and what I have come to realize is that I can't do it on my own. I must have divine help to make it through. I also must keep the focus off myself and on God and His ultimate plan for my life. I may not always have everything I want, but He will always give me what I need and grace and mercy to make it through each day.

Since writing this book, I have met and married my wonderful prince, and we now have four amazing boys. I want to encourage you that it is worth it to wait for that one special man to come into your life and sweep you off your feet. We had both prayed for each other and saved everything for each other. The first kiss on the lips for both of us was each other on our wedding day—in front of all our family and friends and captured on film and video for posterity! While the years I spent as a single woman tried my patience and frustrated me beyond belief, I can see God's hand in it. I still don't completely understand why I had to wait so long for my fairy tale, but I know God is using the experiences I had and the lessons I learned to help me accomplish the things He has me doing even now. And so I encourage you to hold on to the Lord, trust Him to guide you and bring your prince, and wait patiently for Him to do so. It may be a long, hard, trying time right now, but it will be worth it in the end.

I pray that as you read this book and as you wait for your special prince to come that God will ease your heartaches, draw you close to Himself, and give you so much joy in your heart that you can't help but smile every day. Keep trusting, keep praying, and keep believing that God will make your dreams come true as you follow Him and do His will.

Melissa Gayle

Prologue

Cinderella had one dance with Prince Charming, and he fell so much in love with her that he spared no expense to find and marry her.

Sleeping Beauty's prince fought his way into the castle to kiss the beautiful sleeping princess and make her his bride.

A handsome prince took one look at Snow White's "dead" face and couldn't help but break the spell to ride off into the sunset with her.

Wouldn't it be nice if a handsome, charming prince wandered into the life of every single one of us, fell head over heels in love, and insisted upon marriage? But princes don't appear to be wandering about aimlessly, and many of us single princesses are tiring of attending balls and twiddling our thumbs with no prince to show for it. Life has certainly revealed itself to be far removed from any fairy tale, but it also possesses a force far better than any found in a fairy tale. The supernatural often appears in these stories as a fairy, such as Cinderella's fairy godmother, or as a force, such as true love conquering all. Isn't it wonderful that in real life we don't depend on fairy godmothers, wishes on a star, or true love righting all wrong? Instead, we put our faith and trust in the only One who can not only make every dream come true but can also make it better than anything we could ever put into a wish.

The plans God has for each of us far exceed anything we could devise for ourselves. But sometimes, we struggle to see the good in what He's given us. How could He leave me single for this long? Why is it no one wants to marry me? Why haven't all my dreams come true? What is God waiting for anyway? Others try

"

to encourage us with statements such as, "Maybe He's trying to teach you something first," or, "Perhaps the young man isn't ready for marriage yet," or, "You're not the only single girl in the world," or, "Well, people are marrying later in life now." Personally, none of these things encourage me. I don't care how late in life other people are choosing to marry. I don't want to wait any longer. I want to get married now!

But this isn't the right attitude. Even though the "encouraging" statements may not truly encourage all of us, we must remember that God is in control of everything and that He still has a perfect will for each and every one of us *and* that His will for us at this particular moment is that we remain single. However, we must also remember that this could change at any time. Just as Cinderella's fairy godmother suddenly appeared to her and just as the handsome princes suddenly woke Sleeping Beauty and Snow White, one day, in God's timing, *our* lives will change forever.

But what do we do in the meantime? How do we handle the daily struggles of a single princess who wants to marry but has no prince? The world turns to unholy relations outside marriage to bring peace and contentment. Not only does this method not work, it also is not an option, according to the Bible. Where, then, can we turn? What comfort do we have, and what should we do to help us through these single years in a way that glorifies God, accomplishes His purpose in our lives, and carries us through until we finally realize our dreams?

I have faced these questions almost constantly for the past several years. For four years, I lived in a college dorm with girls who met "the one" during our years of rooming together and some who had already met him and were preparing for marriage. One year, out of the eight of us in our suite, five were dating their future husbands. Over the years, I have watched several of my friends marry and start families, and I see more and more of them pair off each year. I am the oldest of three, and my younger sister has already met and married her prince—I always thought the firstborn should marry first. I have cried myself to sleep over my single state more times than I can count, and several times I thought I would die if I were not married or at least dating "the one" extremely soon. But here I am, still alive and still single.

Perhaps you think I'm crazy, an overemotional wreck obsessed with getting married and desperately trying to change her state of singleness. I'll agree to the emotional part, but I'm not obsessed with marriage, and I'm not desperate. I'm also not alone. I know there are many single women in this world who would love to change their single status and, no matter how many horror stories they hear about being married, would give almost anything to try it.

During these past years of having my singleness almost rubbed in my face at every turn, I have learned the answers to the questions previously listed. Where can the single girl turn for comfort and guidance? What instruction can she find that deals with her specific needs, needs that change or intensify with each passing year? I still cry sometimes, more often than I'd like, and I still have moments I think my heart may break, but I know it's not true, and I feel no despair or desperateness. I have joy and peace from God that He is working in my life and will soon bring to pass my dearest dream. This book is for each single princess who believes that one day her dream will come true: her prince will find her and spare no expense to make her his wife.

Until then, we must remain strong in the Lord, but we also must realize that life doesn't wait for marriage before it begins. Life is already here, waiting for us. Happiness doesn't start with a charming prince; it begins with the Prince of Peace. Love doesn't depend on the determination of a prince to find his bride; it flows freely from God above Who gives us all we need to truly live. If we put our lives on hold until we marry, we underestimate not only ourselves but also what God can do through us, perhaps even bring about that marriage we so long for. A storybook life is not given to us, but joy, peace, contentment, happiness, and even love are readily available and waiting for each of us if we learn how to access them.

Truly, life is no fairy tale, but with our faith in God and who He is, we can still live happily ever after.

When Your Dream Doesn't Come True

Scenario

Ever since I can remember, I have dreamed of growing up and getting married. I could hardly wait to meet that perfect guy and marry him. It was my favorite dream. I didn't date a lot in high school—in fact, my first date wasn't until my senior year—but my parents always told me to wait until I got to college. "You'll meet someone there," they said. I took them literally. I imagined myself as a college freshman going to class, getting involved, minding my own business when—suddenly—an upperclassman would approach, dazzled by my beauty, and ask me to have dinner with him. I would agree to dinner with this gorgeous hunk of man, of course. Then, we'd finish college, marry, have children, and live happily ever after. Or something like that.

But none of it happened. I had a few dates, but nothing anywhere near a fairy tale. No Prince Charming stumbled across my path, and I graduated alone. Oh, my family was there, but as far as my marital status, I was alone.

Yet I was not done with college! I pursued a master's degree. *Okay, Lord*, I thought, *perhaps You want more time to make my dream come true.* I didn't stay in order to find a husband, but I considered the prospect within the realm of possibility. It was not to be, and once again, I graduated alone.

My biggest dream from the time I could dream had not come true.

I had completed six years of college training yet remained alone. I felt as though my best friend had perished, for truly my dearest dream had died.

Scripture

To remind us that no matter how forgotten we may feel He has not turned His back on us, God says in Psalm 94:14, "For the Lord will not cast off His people, neither will He forsake His inheritance (KJV)." If we have accepted Jesus Christ as our Savior, then we are part of His people. He will never forsake us.

In Jeremiah 29:11, God promises, "For I know the thoughts that I think toward you, saith the Lord, thoughts of peace, and not of evil, to give you an expected end (KJV)." He Who knows the end from the beginning has planned a good life for each of us. Sometimes it just takes a while to get to the expected end.

Keep the right perspective by reading 2 Corinthians 4:8-10. In the King James version, It says, "We are troubled on every side, yet not distressed; we are perplexed, but not in despair, persecuted, but not forsaken; cast down, but not destroyed; always bearing about in the body the dying of the Lord Jesus, that the life also of Jesus might be made manifest in our body."

Solution

In every book I've ever read about being single and waiting for God's timing for marriage, I'm told to enjoy my single years, to remember that I will never have these opportunities for ministry and service again, and to keep a smile on my face and remember God is in control. All of these statements are true, and the advice is sound: we must use this time for accomplishing whatever it is God wants us to get done. But no one had ever told me how to handle the death of a dream. I didn't even realize how dear a dream could become—until that last graduation. That's when it really hit me that I was alone with no prospective husbands showing interest. That's when I realized my dream wasn't coming true.

When someone close to us dies, we grieve. We mourn the passing of that person for a time; we may shed tears—we may shed many —and feel saddened and melancholy for a while. Then, we either, with God's help, pull ourselves out of the depths of our grief and move on with our lives or wallow in the depths of despair until we join the dearly departed. The same is true for the death of a dream. What no one ever acknowledged in any book I read was that sadness over a dream that didn't come true was a legitimate emotion. We can mourn for a time and allow ourselves to deal with the grief that we feel.

But we must, with God's help, pull ourselves out of mourning and move on with life, or we will wallow in self-pity for the rest of our days. On several occasions, I vented my grief over my loss, but each time, I had to pull out of it, recognize God's sovereignty in my life, rejoice in His workings in my life, and move on, glorifying Him. The key to dealing with the death of a dream is to deal with it and move on; pull out of mourning as soon as possible. No one ever told me I *could* mourn because no one wanted me to stay there. It's not wrong to mourn; it's just wrong to stay there.

There is another side to the death of a dream, however, and that is the birth of a new one. If God allows one dream to die, it is to enable us to pursue a different dream—His dream. Sometimes He makes it very clear what we are to do, and sometimes He takes His time letting us know what specific dream we need to have. The important thing is that we follow His leading, even when we can't see the end of the path or even more than the next step. If we trust Him to take care of our dreams and focus on what He has for us today, we can pull out of mourning and into rejoicing, knowing that God is in control and is working out a beautiful plan for our lives that will draw us closer to Him, bring glory to His name, and eventually make all our dreams come true.

Something Extra...

To Think About

If the Lord is making you wait this long for your prince, then when it happens, it will be better than anything you could ever dream; and when you look back at this time spent waiting, learning, and growing, you'll say, "It was worth it." Because God's will always is.

If it hasn't happened your way, rejoice, for then what does happen will be God's way. If it doesn't happen the logical way, praise God, for then what does happen will be miraculous. If it doesn't happen the way you consider best, be glad, for then what does happen *will be* the best—and the best from God is better than anything we can dream.

To Evaluate

What do the statements above mean to you?

What do Isaiah 55:8-13 and Jeremiah 29:11 tell you? What do they reveal about God's plan for your life?

What blessings has God given you this week? This month? This year?

Besides marriage, what dreams do you have for your life? How many have come true, and how many has God put on hold, for now? Do you trust Him to fulfill them in His time?

To Try

Find a verse specifically about God's sovereignty and claim it as your own by memorizing it, meditating upon it throughout the day, praying it to God, and honestly believing the truth it has to say.

Find a song to help pull you out of mourning and into rejoicing.

Make a list of the dreams that have come true. Use this list to encourage yourself in the Lord.

Make a list of the dreams that have not come true. Pray over each one, giving it to the Lord and thanking Him for giving you His best in that area.

Smile over something good every day.

Go to bed smiling, resting in the Lord.

When You Feel You Can't Go On

Scenario

I was twenty-four years old and had been crying for about ten minutes because of the pressures I felt myself under: moving eighteen hours away from home; nervous about my new home and job; discouraged because of changes in my familial relationships; and lonely because my biggest dream had always been marriage, yet no matter how hard I prayed, I remained glaringly single.

The desire to hold and be held by that special someone who would love me for the rest of his life, at times, overwhelmed me. I cried myself to sleep at night. I cried when my sister's boyfriend did something nice for her. I cried at the drop of a hat for no good reason and with no control over my tear ducts. My eye doctor told me several of my tear glands were "capped over," and my dad hardly believed it because I cried so much! And there I sat again, crying in the bathroom.

My mother had followed me, trying to advise me about my situation—telling me things that I, of course, did not particularly care to hear. Then suddenly, she had tears in her eyes. Why was she crying when I was the one with the problems? She told me she hated to see me upset, and I felt horrible for making my mother cry. And then she said one of the most important things she has ever said to me. She told me that I was God's child whom He had created with a purpose, that I had a job to do for Him, that I had meaning for being here, and that God had been using me to touch people. All of a sudden, I had a reason *not* to cry.

Scripture

Mordecai told Esther, "…who knoweth whether thou art come to the kingdom for such a time as this," Esther 3:9 (KJV). Perhaps the same question could be asked of us.

In Isaiah 41:10, God promises to help and strengthen His children. The verse reads, "Fear thou not; for I am with thee: be not dismayed; for I am thy God: I will strengthen thee; yea, I will help thee; yea, I will uphold thee with the right hand of my righteousness (KJV)."

Acts 22:14-15 says, "And he said, 'The God of our fathers hath chosen thee, that thou shouldest know His will, and see that Just One, and shouldest hear the voice of His mouth. For thou shalt be His witness unto all men of what thou hast seen and heard (KJV).'" God gives us experiences and circumstances to teach us aspects of His character and elements of His will for our good but also so that we may be a witness to others of His grace, mercy, power, and more.

God requires us to take control of our minds. He says, "Casting down imaginations, and every high thing that exalteth itself against the knowledge of God, and bringing into captivity every thought to the obedience of Christ," 2 Corinthians 10:5 (KJV).

Solution

"You touch people," my mother told me through her tears. "God has given you talents and abilities that touch people's lives." It hit me, as I listened to my mother's words and saw the sincerity in her eyes, that what she said was true. God was using my life in the lives of others to affect them for Him.

This was the turning point for me. God wasn't waiting for me to marry in order for me to be effective for His service. He was using me now, in my single state, to perform His work. He was using me just as He used Ruth, Rahab, Esther, Mary, Elizabeth, and Tabitha during the times of the Bible.

Now, you may be thinking, *I've heard this before, and I can't believe you didn't realize you had a purpose.* Well, the truth is, I'd heard it before too, and I knew I had a purpose. But suddenly I realized that *I* had a specific purpose in the eyes of the Lord. He was using *me*, not just the general audience at church, but me specifically, to accomplish His specific purpose. *I* had been created and redeemed by God so that He could give me specific talents and abilities and use them for His glory. *I* am important to God, and I have a job to do.

Now, this may sound arrogant, but it's not. I am important to God, and so are *you*. Yes, in the grand scheme of life, we are insignificant, and God is so much greater than we can ever imagine. But we are important to Him. He has a specific job for me that only I can accomplish; He has a specific job for *you*, the princess reading this book, that only *you* can accomplish.

Perhaps you think, as I did, that God will use you at some point but not now. I tend to think of God using me sometime in the future; I don't think of it as a current thing. And yet, current is exactly what it is. As soon as we become Christians and surrender our wills to God for Him to use for His purposes, He begins to use us. We can't always see it, and we may not always realize exactly how He's using us, but He does if we allow Him—if we stay close to Him and follow His will.

As we realize that God uses us, we face a very real danger. Satan works to stop us from being used by God. He tries every trick he can devise to keep God's children—His princesses—from doing His will. One of the easiest places for Satan to attack us is in our minds. If he can convince us that we are worthless before we marry, that our single state has hindered us from being all that we can be, that we have nothing to live for, and that life is hopeless and depressing, then he can keep us from being used by God. He can drag us down and make us of no use to anyone, least of all a husband!

We must fight Satan and his demons in this direct attack against our minds and service for Christ. We must recognize that our depressing thoughts are not truth; they are lies straight from the devil. We must rally ourselves and put away those awful lies. Each one of us must tell ourselves the truth: God is in control. He has a plan for my life. He has a prince for me and will bring us together as soon as He is ready. I am important to God, and He is using me, now, in my current position, to touch others and to bring glory to Himself and honor to His name. God loves me and always wants the best for me.

Finally, we must smile. Not the sad half-smile we give people who express sympathy for our singleness, but an honest smile. Smile to reflect the joy of the Lord, of serving Him, of being used by Him for His purpose, of sharing His love with others, the joy of experiencing His love personally, and of course, of knowing that He has a special prince out there designed specifically for His princess. That day with my mother, I realized that my life is made up of choices: I have to choose to be happy and to rejoice in the Lord no matter how long I remain single. It is my choice to bring my thoughts into submission that they may not tear me down but may build me up. I must decide to allow God to use me to touch people and to follow Him no matter the heartaches because when they come, I can trust Him to get me through. I must choose to focus on all that God has done for me and not on the few things I want and can't have, yet. I will resolve to live every day now and not wait until someday comes to live. I will let God order my steps and my life, for only then can I truly be happy. Only then can I find peace. Only then can I live happily ever after, even after the slipper fits.

Something Extra...

To Think About

God uses His children in many areas of life. You may work in an office and see the same few people every day, but your attitude and your outlook on life can show them the hope you have within and encourage them, bless them, and even lead them to salvation and a closer walk with God. Don't let Satan convince you that your life touches no one. Your life touches many; touch them for Christ.

People watch you when you are unaware. The clerk at the store observes your attitude. The people at church notice your mannerisms. Those you think have no idea who you are may not know your name, but they know about you. What do they see?

To Evaluate

What do the statements above mean to you?

How can Isaiah 43:10-12 be applied to your life?

How does applying Philippians 4:8-9 affect your thought process?

How has God used you in the past?

How many people do you see each day? Are you affecting them for

Christ?

What has God brought into your life that you never planned? Is He using that to touch others?

To Try

Claim a verse specifically about being used for God.

Find a song to help focus your thoughts on the right things.

Make a list of all the ways you can touch people.

Find someone to encourage. Try to find at least one person a week, or even a day.

Smile over something good every day.

Go to bed smiling, resting in the Lord.

15

When You Want Something More

Scenario

Almost every Saturday, I wake up feeling rather melancholy. Because it's my only day to sleep in, I lie in bed, think of all I must accomplish over the weekend, and dream of being married. Tears sting my eyes as I imagine waking up next to my husband or meeting him at the altar during our wedding or looking up into his face and seeing in his eyes a deep, abiding love for me. I brush the tears off my cheeks and pray for God to help me make it through another day alone and to guide and protect my prince until He brings us together—preferably soon.

Sometimes, I can shake the melancholy mood quickly and move on with my day. Other times, it stays with me through the entire weekend. I start to wonder what's wrong with me. I have a lot going for me—I enjoy my job; I have friends, though many are married or dating; I have a wonderful family—but still I feel something's missing. I know what it is, and I ache to find it. I want to get married. I want to have a husband who loves me more than anything else in the world. I want to make dinner for someone other than myself. I want to come home and tell someone about my day and hear about his and know that no matter what happened during the day, we will always be together and love each other and care for each other. In spite of all the blessings I have been given, there is one I have not. And that is the one I desire the most. I collapse onto my bed and let the tears flow, wondering how I'm supposed to make it through the weekend, let alone the following week.

Scripture

God reminds us to keep our focus on Him. Psalm 37:4-5 says, "Delight thyself also in the Lord; and He shall give thee the desires of thine heart. Commit thy way unto the Lord; trust also in Him; and He shall bring it to pass (KJV)."

Psalm 130:5 states, "I wait for the Lord, my soul doth wait, and in His Word do I hope (KJV)." This verse reminds us that as we wait on God to fulfill our desires, we can find hope in His Word.

Paul's biblical perspective is recorded in Philippians 4:11 which says, "Not that I speak in respect of want: for I have learned, in whatsoever state I am, therewith to be content (KJV)."

We can be content in our circumstances because God has promised to always be with us. Hebrews 13:5 says, "Let your conversation be without covetousness; and be content with such things as ye have: for He hath said, I will never leave thee, nor forsake thee (KJV)."

Solution

Perhaps some would see me lying in tears on my bed and say, "You need to be content with what you have been given. Think of those who have nothing, and look at all you have. Don't wish for more; be content!" This pronouncement sounds extremely harsh. What do you mean I shouldn't wish for more? Is it wrong to want to marry? Am I discontented if I desire something more? The answer is no, but the answer is also to be content. The solution to the problem is contentment, but that doesn't mean I can't desire something other than what I have, as long as that desire is within God's will.

The Bible tells us to be content no matter what. But contentment is not the absence of desires in your heart. When He lived on earth, Jesus desired all men to come to Him and believe. He never fully received the fulfillment of that desire, but I would never say that Jesus was not content, for discontentment is a sin, and He never sinned. Paul desired to tell certain rulers of his day about Jesus but was content before he was able to do so—in other words, he was content before his desire was fulfilled.

Contentment, then, is not the absence of desires. Instead, it is an acceptance of the circumstances we find ourselves in without bitterness or resentment. It is not the lack of hope for something more but rather the presence of peace that for right now, in this moment, you are in the center of God's will, accomplishing His plan for you, and trusting Him to care for the rest. It is knowing *and* accepting that everything God brings or allows in your life is there to mold you into a more perfect likeness of Jesus Christ, working all things for good and for perfection. It is trusting Him to bring to pass all that He has placed in your heart—for if your desire is from Him, He will fulfill it in His time.

Contentment, then, is a daily decision—sometimes an every-moment-of-the-day decision—that you will not despair, become depressed, or wallow in self-pity. It is the decision to give the desire over to God and let Him handle it. If we give Him our desires, He will give us back the desires we should have in our hearts. Some may be the same ones we handed Him originally; others may be new. But all will be from Him, and we can trust that He, then, will bring them to pass. We must decide to trust God and rejoice in every choice He makes, because His will is perfect and His way is right. If we allow Him to fill our hearts with that peace that passes all understanding and with the desires He wants us to have, and if we allow Him to take care of fulfilling those desires, we can live full, complete, contented lives. Only when we are right with God can we find true happiness. Only when we allow Him to give it can we obtain true peace. And only when we rest contentedly in Him can we live happily ever after.

Something Extra...

To Think About

God ordains the circumstances; you control your attitude. Ultimately, you are responsible for how you live your life: blissfully or bitterly.

Contentment is a choice.

To Evaluate

What do the statements above mean to you?

In what areas do you struggle with contentment the most? What can you do to help yourself be more content?

How does Psalm 37:4-5 tell us to be content?

How can Hebrews 13:5 encourage and exhort us in the area of being single? What does it tell you specifically?

Read Psalm 20. What does that passage mean to you in the area of being single?

To Try

Claim a verse specifically about being content or resting in God.

Find a song to help you trust God.

Make a list of all the areas in which you struggle with bitterness; then determine ways to combat those bitter feelings.

Make a list of all your heart's desires; pray about each one specifically, giving it to God, and trusting Him to take care of it.

Smile over something good every day.

Go to bed smiling, resting in the Lord.

When You Wonder Why

Scenario

I notice couples everywhere. I can't escape them no matter what I do. I work with them; I live next door to them; my friends become them; I read about them in books. And I wonder about them. Sometimes, I look at a couple and think, *How did a person who looks like that end up with another person who looks like* that? Other times, I think, *How did a person who acts like that end up married?* I'm not trying to be mean, and I generally keep these thoughts to myself, but I do wonder. I watch the person who never thought about marriage walk down the aisle, and I think, *Why did they get to marry when they were perfectly happy being single and I, who would love to marry, must remain single?*

Then, I look in the mirror. Sometimes, I think, *If I can look like this, why am I not married, yet?* Other times, I think, *If I look like this, no wonder I'm not married!* And when I see the other couples around, sometimes I think, *If that person can find someone to marry, why can't I?*

None of these thoughts are healthy, or even necessarily true, but they do enter my mind and provoke me to wonder why. Why am I still single? Why hasn't it worked out for me yet? Am I doing something wrong? Am I not right with God? Is there something wrong with me? Why have so many others found the one thing that I long for, and why can't I find it?

Scripture

We are not the only ones who have struggled with feelings of despair. David offers his admonition to his dejected soul in Psalm 42: 5 which says, "Why art thou cast down, O my soul? And why art thou disquieted in me? Hope thou in God: for I shall yet praise Him for the help of His countenance (KJV)."

Jeremiah offers this suggestion in Jeremiah 30:15. It says, "Why criest thou for thine affliction? Thy sorrow is incurable for the multitude of thine iniquity: because thy sins were increased, I have done these things unto thee (KJV)."

Micah reminds us that God wants to gather us to Himself. Micah 4:12 reads, "But they know not the thoughts of the Lord, neither understand they His counsel: for He shall gather them as the sheaves into the floor (KJV)."

Paul warns against bitterness in Hebrews 12:15, which says, "Looking diligently lest any man fail of the grace of God; lest any root of bitterness springing up trouble you, and thereby many be defiled (KJV)."

Solution

The answer to these questions may not be pleasant to hear because much of it we have heard before and because even knowing the answer cannot immediately resolve the issue. The truth boils down to God's will. He is the One who knows what is best for each of us and when it is the best time for us to have what we desire.

God's will is different for everyone. For some, He brings marriage early in their lives while others must wait. Some people get married first and then decide what career to pursue and where to live and what to dedicate their lives to doing; others do the reverse. Many follow God's plan for their lives concerning marriage; others take it into their own hands. Those who follow God's plan are blessed by Him; those who try to run their lives on their own are not, though they may appear to be for a time.

No matter how many people marry before we do, we can rest assured that God has not forgotten us or left us hanging. He just has something better for us than what we dreamed for ourselves. His timing for our marrying is perfect, no matter what our earthly minds believe. It's hard to see others marry and start families —seemingly unbearable at times—but just because it hasn't happened for us yet doesn't mean it's not going to. God doesn't give us desires to torture us. When we surrender our will to Him, He gives us the desires He wants us to have in order to bring honor and glory to His name. Thus, if He's given you the desire to marry, relax and trust Him to fulfill that desire in His time. Don't rush into a relationship out of desperation or give yourself to a man you're not married to. Wait on the Lord, and He will bring His best for you in His time.

A word of encouragement: fight bitterness and resentment. Watching so many people obtain the one thing you desire is incredibly difficult, but fight bitterness with all your might, if only for the reason that no one wants to marry a bitter, resentful woman. Bitterness will consume your life, hinder your walk with Christ, hurt your friendships, and kill your chances of finding a charming prince. Remember that God loves you more than even you love yourself. He wants you to be happy, and He wants you to be happy in Him. He only has your best interest in mind, and even if you don't understand it all, trust that His will is always best for you.

Now, it is true that the crux of the matter is God's will. It is also true that we have a part in His will. We must remain right with

God in order to know where He's leading us and be able to follow Him. We don't always know why God chooses a certain path for us, but if we follow Him no matter where He leads, we can always be certain that the path is for us and that He will care for and provide for us all along the way. I've heard of several cases where God led the individual away from her comfort zone and into a new place, and within a year, she had found her prince. I'm not saying we all need to move in order to marry, but we do need to follow wherever God leads in order for His will to be accomplished in our lives. And in order for us to know His leading, we must remain right with Him.

Some people say that single people remain single because they have some sin in their lives that they need to take care of. It is foolish to make such a blanket statement; it is also foolish to automatically disregard it. Indeed, it is not for others to automatically judge based on circumstances, as Job's friends did in the book of Job in the Bible; however, as Job did have the sin of pride, we must evaluate our own lives to determine if we do have sin blocking our fellowship with God. If we do, we must confess it to God, ask for forgiveness, turn from it, and move on.

Other people believe that single people remain single because they haven't learned to be satisfied or content with God alone. I find this to be a rather interesting argument for many reasons. First, I don't like being told that just because I'm single, I must have a problem with contentment. Second, I don't believe the statement to be universally true—while it's true for some, perhaps even a majority, it is not true of every single girl. Third, being satisfied with God alone is not something that we can only learn during our single years; indeed, no matter our marital status, we must always find our satisfaction and contentment in God alone for that is what He desires of us.

However, I do believe the argument has some merit, in that for us to be happy and content throughout our lives, we must look to Christ for everything. He should be the first person we turn to when things go wrong. He should be the first One we rejoice with when things go well. He is the answer to every problem we face, and He is the only One who will never let us down, forget a promise or a special occasion, or turn His back on us. As much as we desire to marry, marriage will not make us happy. It may satisfy that specific desire, but if we think a husband is going to be able to satisfy all of our desires, we are destined for a miserable life. Our only complete satisfaction is found in God alone. No matter who the husband is, he will never satisfy every desire. Only God can do that, and—praise God!—He will if we ask Him.

My mom tells me all the time that men are not like the men I read about in my romance novels, with the exception of my dad. My dad, according to my mom, is an exceptional man—the most wonderful man on earth (and watching my dad over the years, I'm inclined to agree with my mom!). But in spite of his exceptional qualities, he cannot satisfy every need my mom has. She's the one who told me a woman's satisfaction can only come from God: trusting Him, having faith in Him, asking for and receiving His love, encouragement, strength, peace, hope, patience, fulfillment, instruction, guidance, correction, forgiveness, and acceptance. His unconditional love and through-the-blood acceptance and fulfillment are perhaps some of the greatest gifts we princesses can ever receive. He's greater than any ring encircling the third finger of the left hand, and He's greater than any man He created could or will ever be. Once that ring is on your finger and your prince carries you off to his castle, don't forget your greatest happiness and contentment do come from God alone.

Something Extra…

To Think About

If your heart is set on doing God's will, and you remain open to Him and right with Him, fear not. He will lead you where He wants you to go, and one day, He'll lead you to the prince He's created especially for you.

To Evaluate

What does the statement above mean to you?

What desires and needs do you have that you feel could only be satisfied by a husband? How many of them can God fulfill?

What problems do you have that you're waiting for marriage to solve? What can you do to solve them now?

What expectations do you have for your prince? Without lowering biblical standards, what expectations do you have that may not be realistic?

What do you learn in Psalm 42? How can you apply it to your own life?

What does Ephesians 2:14 mean to you?

To Try

Claim a verse specifically about God's care of you.

Find a song to help you rely on God.

Make a list of the qualities you expect in your prince. Keep the list as short and as realistic as possible. Pray about each quality you put on your list.

Make a list of every need you feel in your life. Ask God to fulfill each one in His way and in His time.

Smile over something good every day.

Go to bed smiling, resting in the Lord.

When You Feel Trapped in the Tower

Scenario

Sometimes I think I must be under a spell or locked in the tower of the castle and not know it. I'm trapped; I'll be single forever. What's happened to my prince? What's taking so long? I have often heard talk about "remaining in the castle," meaning to not run off with the first nice guy who catches your eye but to wait for the prince God has for you. I half joke to myself that I don't even have the opportunity to leave the castle, let alone actually run off with someone. Why do I feel so trapped?

Other times, I have no feelings of entrapment. Instead, I feel rather satisfied with what the Lord has given me, and I feel confident that He will bring a prince my way at any time. The world seems rose colored and beautiful, and life is just wonderful.

Why do my emotions fly all over the place? Why do I feel in despair one day and in euphoria the next? And when I do feel life is wonderful, why can't I hold on to that feeling and keep it forever? What am I supposed to do?

Scripture

Focusing our minds on the right thing is our responsibility, and the Bible tells us how to accomplish this task. Proverbs 16:3 says, "Commit thy works unto the Lord, and thy thoughts shall be established (KJV)." The Bible also says in 2 Corinthians 10:5, "Casting down imaginations, and every high thing that exalteth itself against the knowledge of God, and bringing into captivity every thought to the obedience of Christ (KJV)."

Ecclesiastes 3:1 and 4 remind us that there are times for every emotion. They say, "To every thing there is a season, and a time to every purpose under the heaven…a time to weep, and a time to laugh; a time to mourn, and a time to dance (KJV)."

The Bible tells us to focus our thoughts on the truth, avoiding the lies of the devil. Philippians 4:8-9 reads, "Finally, brethren, whatsoever things are true, whatsoever things are honest, whatsoever things are just, whatsoever things are pure, whatsoever things are lovely, whatsoever things are of good report; if there be any virtue, and if there be any praise, think on these things. Those things, which ye have both learned, and received, and heard, and seen in me, do: and the God of peace shall be with you (KJV)."

Solution

Life, especially for women, can be an emotional rollercoaster. Often, our feelings can change within a moment. These emotional changes are normal for most of us; because of this, we must recognize these changes and work to pull ourselves out of the depths of despair. No matter what we look like or who we are, none of us are locked in the tower of the castle. We all have the same loving Father who brings only the best for His children.

Our responsibility, then, is to remember this fact. When we feel desperate or alone, we must rally our spirits and encourage ourselves in the Lord. We must remind ourselves that life is dynamic, God's will is perfect, He has a fantastic plan for each of us, and the best part of that plan may happen today. And if it doesn't, well, tomorrow is another day. It's not easy to live day after day and hope something happens soon, but God is faithful to help and encourage and give us strength to pull out of the doldrums and carry on.

We will go through times of trials and sadness, and God never tells us not to cry. But He does say there is a time for it. God understands our emotional upheavals—He must, for He created us this way—but God never planned for us to stay sad or to live in a constant state of tears. So when all we want to do is cry in the corner, what can we do to pull ourselves out of this state?

First, we can pray. Ask the Lord for help, and tell Him all about your longings and desires and how sad you feel because they have not yet been fulfilled. He is the only One who never tires of hearing from us, even about the same problem continually. He's also the only One who can do anything about our longings and desires. Who better to tell than the One who understands, cares, and can satisfy all our longings?

Second, we can read the Bible. I know this sounds trite, but truly the best encouragement and help in the world is found within the pages of God's Holy Word. He gave us the manual for handling all that life brings. It is the greatest source of comfort and encouragement I have ever found, because it shows me how the One who can handle all my problems will do so and what I am supposed to do in relation to all my problems.

Third, we can watch what we feed our minds. I must admit that I absolutely adore love stories. Christian romance novels are my favorite books, and happily-ever-after movies are the best. Most of the time, I can handle romance novels and love stories, but there are times when I know if I watch or read the story, I'll do nothing but cry and feel sorry for myself. When that happens, I try to make myself watch or read something else, something encouraging or uplifting or just not related to getting married. I often listen to music that encourages me with the message that one day my dream will come true.

My absolute favorite story is *Cinderella.* Even though I'm not waiting for a wish to come true but for my prayer to the Lord to be fulfilled, I still find the tale of this good little girl being rewarded for her sweet spirit and getting to marry the prince to be very encouraging. That's what we have to do: find good, decent, wholesome things that help us feel happy—songs we like to hear, books we like to read, movies we like to watch, pictures we like to look at—and make provision for our emotions to be uplifted, encouraged, and gladdened in the Lord.

Something Extra...

To Think About

When you feel trapped in the tower, look at all God's done for you: He's loved you; He's provided for you; He paid the ultimate price for you. Now look further, at what else He's done—personal blessings He's given you, situations He's worked together for your good and His glory, impossibilities He's somehow made possible. With all that He's done for you and all He's invested in your life to bring you to Him and to use you for His glory, do you honestly think He'll deny you His best—especially regarding the divine ordinance of marriage? How can you *not* trust the Lord?

To Evaluate

What does the statement above mean to you?

How does Psalm 139:17-18 speak to you?

What does 2 Corinthians 10:5 mean to you?

What do you feed your mind that provokes you to sadness, particularly over your singleness? How often do you feast on these things?

What do you feed your mind that encourages or inspires you? How often do you feast on these things?

To Try

Claim a verse specifically to encourage yourself in the Lord.

Find a song to encourage yourself in the Lord.

Read an uplifting book.

Make a list of those desires or needs that trap you the most. Tell God about each need specifically and listen for His response, through either a verse or that still, small voice. Find a verse to deal with each need, and write it down next to each one. In your own words, write down how the verse deals with the problem. Consult your list when you struggle with that problem to remind yourself that God is taking care of that need.

Smile over something good every day.

Go to bed smiling, resting in the Lord.

When Townsfolk Rub It In

Scenario

It never failed. Every time I returned from college, the same question faced me: "So, do you have anybody special down there?" The answer every single time was, "No." Sometimes, I tried to be creative: "I'm waiting for him to get right with the Lord. He must need a lot of work before we can meet." The response from the questioner was pretty similar each time: a disappointed look and a statement. These statements ranged from, "What's wrong with those guys down there?" (my favorite!) to "You know, it happens at different times for everyone," to "God has someone special for you, and you just have to wait for His timing," to "You've got to get out there, girl, and be available!" Every questioner only had my best interest at heart, and no one meant to rub it in, but they did.

Each time I faced this situation, I had just been through one of the hardest times for me as a single college student. My college required attendance at certain concerts, plays, and programs. Most people used these events as a dating opportunity. Thus, most in attendance were paired off—not really a fun experience for one who attended with a few girls or alone. One of these required events occurred at the end of every semester. With me, then, coming from an emotional event where my singleness had been somewhat rubbed in, I truly didn't feel encouraged when I returned home to questions specifically about my state of singleness. Again, everyone meant well, and no one meant to rub it in, but they did.

Family would question me and give me advice. "Get out there," "Don't just go to your room and do homework; meet people and go to activities with them," "Be sure you look nice, and take care of yourself," and, "Be friendly." I took their advice; nothing changed. Each time someone advised me concerning my appearance or my activities, it felt as though they were blaming me for being single, as if I were killing my chances of getting married by something I did or did not do.

With all these people advising me out of concern for my terrifyingly single state, I felt overwhelmed. I already put enough pressure on myself because I had no special someone, and then I found reminders everywhere I went. I couldn't handle it, but what could I do? These people all cared about me, but I was about to break down. *Was* my being single actually my fault? And how could it be if I followed everyone's advice? What in the world was I supposed to do?

Scripture

No matter what is being said, we are admonished to exercise restraint, exhibiting godliness and Christ-like behavior. Romans 12:12 says, "Be kindly affectioned one to another with brotherly love, in honour preferring one another; not slothful in business; fervent in spirit; serving the Lord; rejoicing in hope; patient in tribulation; continuing instant in prayer (KJV)."

Along those same lines, 1 Thessalonians 5:14 tells us, "…be patient toward all men (KJV)."

No matter what people may say to us while we are there, simply refusing to attend church services is not the right solution. God admonishes us in Hebrews 10:25, "Not forsaking the assembling of ourselves together, as the manner of some is; but exhorting one another: and so much the more, as ye see the day approaching (KJV)."

Solution

These situations are rather difficult to deal with because there are many considerations: our feelings, the questioner's feelings, the care or love we have for and the desire not to be mean or rude to the questioner, and, of course, the fact that no matter how many times the question is posed, the advice is given, or the advice is taken, we still remain single. With all these considerations to take into account, this solution is neither easy nor simple. Nonetheless, it is possible to be happy in the midst of, or perhaps even in spite of, these well-meaning townsfolk who unknowingly rub it in.

This solution, as with most solutions, begins on the inside. We never like to hear it, but it's true: the first place for change to begin is always within ourselves. In this situation, the first step is recognizing that the question stems from a caring heart. The person asking questions wants to know that we're happy and that we're being taken care of. They see marriage as the natural step for a single girl to take in order to be happy and provided for in this life. They may also see it as the blessing of God that it is and want our lives to be blessed by Him in that way—much as we ourselves do. Their motive in asking is to see that we are happy and blessed. Of course, we've already learned that we can be happy and blessed without being married, but most townsfolk don't realize this. We can show them by how we live and conduct ourselves, but there will be some who never fully understand.

After we recognize that their motive is good, we still must deal with the rotten way we feel when we're asked the questions. Pray for help. If you know you're going where you'll have to deal with these questions, pray before you go. Then pray while you're there and facing the situation. God is mighty and full of strength; He will help you through if you ask Him.

Now, we've seen their motive is good, and we've prayed for help. The next step is to answer the question as quickly as possible and change the subject. Most of the time, if I answer the question politely and change the subject, people follow my lead. I tell myself that I can think about it and cry about it later when I'm alone. While I'm there, I force my mind to think about something else, because I know if I don't I won't make it through the conversation.

Dealing with family, however, can be a bit different. Generally, family is with us more than townsfolk are, and our families see the things we hide from the rest of the world. My mother and my sister know more about my personal struggle with singleness than do the ladies at my church. Because of this more personal relationship, I can talk more candidly with them, especially about the advice that they gave me.

I actually told my mother and my sister that statements such as, "You're not the only one who's single—look at the other single girls around you," and, "People are marrying later in life these days," and, "When it's time, he'll be there," didn't really help me feel any better about being single and alone. I also told them—as kindly as I could—that telling me to get out there and be friendly and take care of myself made me feel as though they were blaming me for remaining single, as though I were responsible for my single state, and as though I wasn't being friendly or taking care of myself. They, of course, assured me that was not their intent, and I knew it wasn't. But because of our familial relationship, I could tell them directly how their comments made me feel. They, in turn, understood and stopped saying most of those statements. My family still gives me some advice, but they have lessened the frequency of the giving.

Now, it's probable that most of those who "rub it in" do so inadvertently and with the best of intentions, but it's also possible that some townsfolk actually try to be cruel and mean. God still sends patience and help and love to endure such things. The Bible says, in Romans 12:21, "Be not overcome of evil, but overcome evil with good." I believe that this is a hard practice. Rarely do we enjoy letting things go and trusting God to take care of the rest, but that is exactly what we need to do. Just as God is in control of everything else, He is in control of those mean people. Handle them the same way you would those who mean well, if you can, and if you can't, comfort yourself with this verse from Romans 12:19: "Vengeance is mine; I will repay, saith the Lord." Leave the vengeance to God—He can destroy enemies much better than you or I can! And when you're hurting from an encounter with an enemy, try praying the Psalms. Some suggestions are Psalms 52, 61, 77, and 94—to name a few.

If you have people pressuring you about getting married, you can't expect the pressure to stop, but you can prepare yourself to face it and survive. God gives strength for every situation; He will not hand you more than you can handle with His help. If you try to face it without Him, however, you will fail miserably. Remind yourself that it is not the townsfolk's opinions that matters and that no matter what they say or who they blame, God is still in control and will make your dream come true in His time. Remind yourself that their advice doesn't mean you are to blame or that you're in the wrong; it simply means they care and they probably don't know what else to say. Bathe the entire experience in prayer. Seek God's face, rely solely on Him, and you can live happily amid the lack of fairy tale.

Something Extra...

To Think About

I know that God always keeps His promises, even if it takes a long time for Him to do so, but others around me may not know this quality of God. For some, their only knowledge of God comes from watching me and listening to what I say about Him. In light of this fact, I must realize that if I tell them that God will provide for my needs, including my need for a husband, but then grow impatient and bitter because I'm still single, I throw doubt on God's reputation and undermine the testimony I gave of Him. In short, I hurt the name of my God. If I have faith enough to say it, I need to have the self-discipline enough to back it up and keep my feelings and emotions in line. But I don't just sit and do nothing. I continue to petition the God of heaven for that which I deeply desire, and I trust Him to bring it to pass for His honor and glory—and for His name's sake.

To Evaluate

What does the statement above mean to you?

What do Romans 12:12 and 1 Thessalonians 5:12-14 tell you?

What "encouraging" statements have you heard lately? What truth can you find in them? What was the heart of the townsperson's question? How can you handle this person next time?

What advice have you been given lately? What advice have you already applied? What else could you apply?

Who has been giving you advice? Is there anyone trying to encourage you that you could politely ask to pray for you instead of commenting?

What situations are the hardest for you in dealing with townsfolk? What mind-set could you have going into the situation that will help you handle it? What topics could you have ready to use to change the direction of the conversation?

Are you thinking kind thoughts about those who care about you and don't realize their questions and advice don't encourage you?

To Try

Claim a verse specifically to calm yourself in these situations.

Find a song to help you keep your focus.

Make a list of every person who gives you advice or encouragement. Write down what you think is the person's motivation for advising or encouraging you. Thank God for bringing each person into your life. If any have mean motives, ask God to help you deal with them.

Think through proper responses for the questions you know you'll be asked the next time you see certain individuals.

Smile over something good every day.

Go to bed smiling, resting in the Lord.

When Couples Surround You

Scenario

For about a month, I could not make it through a Sunday night church service without crying at least once. As much as I wished I could refrain from tearing up, I could not keep my eyes dry to save my life. I attended Sunday night church services with two of my college friends. One of them was about to get married. Needless to say, that was slightly rough on the ~~other~~ two of us who weren't even dating anyone.

But the friend getting married was only the beginning of my emotional trek through the church services. We would sit in a less-occupied section of the balcony, a section that somehow seemed to always have couples sitting between me and the preacher. All I could see in front of me were these couples sharing hymnals and whispering back and forth. If I looked to the side, I saw my friend's sparkling engagement ring. Even the songs we sang seemed to speak of love and such. Everywhere I looked I saw reminders that I was alone. I couldn't take it. I cried every week.

I went home for the summer and discovered that it only got worse at church there. At least at college, one of my friends was still single with me. At home, I was completely surrounded: I sat in the pew with my parents on one side (they may be my parents, but they're still a married couple) and my sister and her boyfriend on the other. I felt quite conspicuous. The couples on either side of me sat close to each other, and I stayed balanced in between them. Alone. All I could think was how nice it would be to have someone to sit close to and share a hymnal with. All I could see was what I didn't have but desired so much. I had tears in my eyes constantly.

And it didn't stop at church. My sister's boyfriend visited her often at our house, and I had nowhere to go. He brought her flowers; he went out to eat with us; he made her smile and laugh. Oh, how I wished I had someone to do that for me! I struggled to keep from crying so much. He did something nice for my sister once when we were eating out, and I had to run to the bathroom to try to mop my eyes before I made a huge display at the table. Making it through the summer was becoming one of the hardest things for me to accomplish.

Then, I faced a new torture: my sister's boyfriend was coming on our family vacation with us (and staying in his own lockout unit). With him there, every single member of my family would be paired off except my brother and me, and my brother, who lived where we were going, was going to be in school most of the time. I was going to be the odd man out for an entire week—the week I was supposed to relax and enjoy. How was I ever going to survive?

Scripture

God promises that if we trust Him, He will shield us. He says, "But let all those that put their trust in Thee rejoice: let them ever shout for joy, because Thou defendest them: let them also that love Thy Name be joyful in Thee. For Thou, Lord, wilt bless the righteous; with favour wilt Thou compass him as with a shield," Psalm 5:11-12 (KJV).

He says that we can run to Him for protection and help. Psalm 94:22 tells us, "But the Lord is my defense; and my God is the rock of my refuge (KJV)."

God also promises us that He will hear our prayers. He says in Psalm 102:17, "He will regard the prayer of the destitute, and not despise their prayer (KJV)."

No matter what our circumstances are, they do not compare to what the Lord endured for us. Keeping in mind what He endured for us and reminding ourselves that we are here to worship Him can keep us from living in depression or despair because of our current single status. 2 Corinthians 4:8-10 says, "We are troubled on every side, yet not distressed; we are perplexed, but not in despair; Persecuted, but not forsaken; cast down, but not destroyed; Always bearing about in the body the dying of the Lord Jesus, that the life also of Jesus might be made manifest in our body (KJV)."

Solution

The main solution I have found to the problem of being surrounded by couples is prayer—not that the couples will disappear but that I will be able to handle myself in spite of their presence. I begin with prayer before I ever get to church or wherever I'm going. I continue with prayer as I endure the event surrounded by couples. I finish with prayer as I attempt to get away from the couples by leaving the event.

Now, I'm not bitter at the couples, and they have done nothing to me personally. I'm just trying to survive my emotional turmoil during this riotous stage of life called singleness. I'm glad the couples have found each other—I can't wait to personally become half of a couple. However, I do find it difficult to be surrounded by couples for extended periods of time. Thus, I pray.

Then, I change the subject. My mind likes to focus on my singleness and get me so worked up that I can't help but bawl. I must force it to concentrate on the sermon or the speaker or some other topic besides my being single in order to get through the event in one piece. Sometimes, though, the thing that actually helps me endure it is picturing myself with my husband at the event. "How will we sit in church?" I ask myself. "Holding hands? His arm around me? Sharing a Bible or using our own?" Often, I couple my musings with prayers for my husband, wherever he is. Many times, God has helped me make it through the services and events without losing control in spite of the couples.

But then, He sent me one of the biggest challenges I could face: vacation surrounded by couples, a vacation of no escape. It would be couples nearly twenty-four hours a day. I couldn't even imagine surviving it, yet I knew that somehow I had to. Going on the vacation was going to be tough, but staying home from it was out of the question.

I began my survival plan months before the anticipated vacation. As soon as I knew the situation, I began praying for God's help to make it through without much emotional toil. I needed a vacation, not a crying fest. I prayed that He would help my heart, that He would keep me from crying too much, and that He would help me not to feel left out during the week. That was my plea before and during the trip.

God answered my prayers and made that vacation one of the best I'd had in years. I spent time with my sister and her boyfriend without crying. I even spent time alone without crying. I spent time with my family without feeling left out or even too single. Oh, I still struggled with my emotions, but not as much as usual. And when it got really hard, I pictured myself coming back on vacation with my husband. I tried to imagine what we would enjoy doing together and how we would interact together with the rest of my family. It's a bittersweet practice, that of imagining the future with that special someone. But the prayers and the daydreams helped me make it through the vacation with only a few moments of difficulty here and there. I considered it a resounding success—one I hope to never have to repeat, but if necessary, one I feel I could.

Only with God's help can we make it through the difficult moments of life, such as attending events that surround you with couples, but praise God, for He gives us what we need to make it through successfully and, yes, even happily.

Something Extra...

To Think About

According to the Bible, Jesus understands everything we experience. His plan for His marriage, however, is not directed at one person but at the church, the bride of Christ. The church, though, is made up of people, every individual who accepts Jesus as his Savior. Once the church is complete, or all those who will accept Him have done so, Jesus can meet His bride, and we will join Him at the marriage supper of the Lamb. Jesus desires His creation to accept Him as Savior and become part of His bride. His desire for all men to come to Him is greater by far than any smidgen of yearning we may feel for one man. In this way, then, Jesus understands our desires and our yearning and our loneliness. In fact, He pleads for men to come to Him more than we ever could for one man. He truly feels our pain and carries our sorrows.

To Evaluate

What does the statement above mean to you?

How does Psalm 6 speak to you in regard to being single? What encouragement can you receive from those verses?

What does 2 Corinthians 4:8-10 tell you about what your mind-set should be? What else does it tell you?

What do the verses in Psalm 94 mean to you? How about Hebrews 13:5b?

What situations will you face in which you will be surrounded by couples? What can you do to handle yourself without breaking down?

To Try

Claim a verse specifically about God's protection and strength.

Find a song to uplift you in spite of the couples.

Try a new mind-set: Try thinking of these couples in a detached manner. Consider every friend who marries as one less person to be concerned for when you get married. Thank God for bringing them together, and pray for Him to bring you together with yours as well. Pray this prayer each time you see the couple.

Smile over something good every day.

Go to bed smiling, resting in the Lord.

When You Feel Stuck Under a Spell

Scenario

What felt like the worst two weeks of my life began with my birthday. It was Monday, and I was moving from Florida to Virginia at the end of the week. My belongings had already been packed and put on a truck. My family and close friends were miles away in other states, and I, for the first time ever, was alone on my birthday. I treated myself to dinner and dessert—take out, of course—and spent the night on an air mattress in my empty apartment with only the television for company. The few years prior, when family had not been close by, I had at least had a friend or two to celebrate with. But this year, I was on my own. I forced myself not to cry—after all, I would be back with family at the end of the week—but I had never felt so lonely.

One week later, I celebrated my birthday again, this time in Virginia with my whole family. I tried to be upbeat as I answered everybody's questions. "Sure, I'm excited to be living with my parents again." "Yes, I'm looking forward to a relaxing summer." "No, I still haven't met anyone special." But as the week continued, reality plagued me with questions I couldn't answer. I couldn't afford to move out, but how long would I need to live with my parents? I never had any desire for a career, but what kind of job should I try to find? My desire was to meet my prince and start a family, but there was no happily-ever-after in sight. Every day was an emotional rollercoaster. My mind switched from a God-will-take-care-of-everything mindset to a no-one-will-ever-love-me mindset in a flash. I laughed; I cried. I was on top of the world and then in the depths of despair. I had moved because I felt God leading me away from that job. Why did God lead me away? What was His purpose for my life? Did He want me to live at home forever? As far as I could see, there would be no end to my misery.

Scripture

God has given us the Bible to help guide us through our lives. Psalm 119:105 says, "Thy word is a lamp unto my feet, and a light unto my path (KJV)."

The book of Psalms reminds us to follow the commandments of the Lord at all times. It says, "I have inclined mine heart to perform thy statutes always, even unto the end," Psalm 119:112 (KJV).

Psalm 16:9 says, "Therefore my heart is glad, and my glory rejoiceth: my flesh also shall rest in hope (KJV)." We can rest in the hope that God has a plan for us, and He will bring it to pass.

Following God's plan ultimately brings peace and joy. Psalm 16:11 says, "Thou wilt show me the path of life: in thy presence is fullness of joy; at thy right hand there are pleasures for evermore (KJV)."

Solution

That first week in Virginia was emotionally horrendous for me. I felt as if I were stuck under a spell that kept me in limbo between the job I had just left and whatever life I was supposed to have with a husband and children of my own in the future. I had no goals and no plans past the summer break. All I knew was that God had moved me home.

But that was all I needed to know. If I had done what God told me to do, then I needed to wait on Him to present the next step for me to take. God doesn't give us all the answers at once; He prefers to teach us to trust Him one step at a time. Trying to handle our frustrations in the meantime, however, can be a challenge. I still had to figure out what I was supposed to do for a job or career, and I was still going to be living with my parents indefinitely.

The solution, this time, was for me to set small, attainable goals for myself. I decided to take the summer to try out a home-based business. If that didn't take off by August, I would look for a job elsewhere. Next, I determined not to worry about moving out for one year. At the end of the year, I would reevaluate my financial standing to see if I could move out. Mentally, I also told myself not to worry about looking for potential husbands until the fall, with plans to tell myself in the fall not to worry about it until after Christmas.

Setting these short-term goals released the tension of the unknown future and allowed me to enjoy each day as it came and concentrate on what each season brought into my life. Thus, I was able to focus on getting my business up and running. I spent time with my family and cultivated those relationships. I used the time I had to work on things besides looking for a prince. Without a husband and family to take care of, I had time to write this book, act in dramatic performances, get involved in ministry projects, and other things that took up my time and energy but were profitable for God's work. Just because I didn't know God's ultimate plan for my life yet, didn't mean I couldn't be used of Him in the meantime. After all, the meantime is part of God's plan, too.

Something Extra...

To Think About

When we follow God's leading, we can trust that we are right where He wants us to be. He doesn't often show us more than one step at a time, but when we follow that step, we can trust Him to show us the next one in His time.

Elijah, in 1 Kings 19, told the Lord that he was the only one left who still believed in God and not Baal. God told Elijah that He still had seven thousand faithful followers in Israel. Sometimes, we may feel as though we're the only ones left without a husband or a family, still waiting on God to bring that answer to our prayers. In reality, we are not alone. There are many faithful followers of Christ patiently waiting on Him to fulfill their deepest desires for marriage. Just as Elijah was not alone, we are not alone.

To Evaluate

What do the statements above mean to you?

What goals can you set for yourself to accomplish now?

What does God want you to do for Him while you are still single?

What relationships do you already have that could be strengthened? What can you do to help strengthen them?

What is God using you to do for Him right now?

What do you hope to accomplish with your life?

To Try

Claim a verse specifically about God's guidance.

Find a song to encourage yourself that God's timing is perfect.

Get involved in something that uses your time and talents to glorify God.

Set short-term and long-term goals for yourself.

Write down ways that God is using you to help others. Rejoice over each one.

Smile over something good every day

Go to bed smiling, resting in the Lord.

When Your Fairy Godmother Appears

Scenario

"You need to get on the internet and register with one of those matchmaking sites—not tomorrow, not next week, today!"

"I have the perfect man for you! He works at the post office, lives with the pastor of his church, and wants to get married. Can I give him your number?"

"There's a couple of guys at my church who are single and interested in marriage. They're a little younger than you are, but that doesn't matter, right? When can you come visit my church and meet them?"

I had barely been back in my hometown a week, and already I was getting advice and offers of arranged meetings to help me meet my prince. The support was overwhelming, but I was a bit concerned. Internet dating makes me nervous, though I do have several friends who have used internet dating sites successfully. And when it comes to blind dates, I don't mind meeting new people, but it concerns me to know so little about someone except that they want to get married.

On the other hand, what if God wants to use a blind date or an internet date to help me meet my prince? Could one of these people offering to set me up on a date actually be my fairy godmother telling me to go to the ball?

Scripture

God has given Christians His Spirit to live within them. The Bible says, "That he would grant you, according to the riches of his glory, to be strengthened with might by his Spirit in the inner man; That Christ may dwell in your hearts by faith; that ye, being rooted and grounded in love," Ephesians 3:16-17 (KJV).

The Holy Spirit within us comforts us and stays with us forever. John 14:16 says, "And I will pray the Father, and he shall give you another Comforter, that he may abide with you for ever (KJV)."

Our Comforter gives us guidance to know God's will for our lives. Jesus said in John 15:26, "But when the Comforter is come, whom I will send unto you from the Father, even the Spirit of truth, which proceedeth from the Father, he shall testify of me (KJV)."

Solution

I hate to say it, but it's true: Fairy godmothers are not real. As far as I can tell from the Bible, God did not give us fairy godmothers. He did, however, give Christians His Holy Spirit to live within us and give us guidance with that still, small Voice. So while we won't have a magical fairy dressing us up to send us to a ball, we do have a miraculous Spirit guiding us to the right place at the right time to finally meet that prince. Sometimes, the Holy Spirit uses friends to introduce two people to each other. He may, also, use an internet dating site to bring two believers together. As long as we follow His prompting, we can trust that He will work His "magic," or His plan, in His time.

Now, some advocate that there is no perfect person for anyone but that merely consulting God on the matter and choosing to love someone else is how Christians should decide to marry. I beg to differ. I agree that no one is perfect, love is a choice, and we should talk to God about the choice we want to make. But if God can call missionaries to a specific mission field, and God can call pastors to a specific church, why can't God bring a specific man and woman together in marriage? I believe that God has a very specific plan for each individual and that if each of us will follow His leading, we will fulfill all that He has for us. I further believe that if we stray from His will, we can repent and be restored to a place of fellowship with Him and still be used of God to accomplish His purpose. On the other hand, I do not believe that we need to be so scared of marrying the wrong person that we never agree to marry anyone. If we stay close to God by reading His Word, praying to Him, listening for His still small Voice, and striving to obey Him, He will not lead us astray. He will make plain the path we should take and give clear guidance for what we should do, whom we should or should not date, and eventually, whom we should marry.

What, then, do we do when faced with blind dates, internet matchmakers, and the like? Follow the prompting of the Holy Spirit. He knows if the blind date is a good idea or not because He knows the future. He knows if we should register with an internet dating site or if that will only lead to trouble. If He gives us peace about going on the date or getting on the internet, then we should absolutely do so, but if He gives us an uneasy feeling about it, we should stay away. Putting ourselves in a situation we were warned against can only lead to trouble and heartache; following the prompting of the Holy Spirit can only lead to peace with God, and perhaps, one day, that happily ever after.

Something Extra…

To Think About

God used Naomi to prompt Ruth to address the subject of marriage with Boaz. God used the act of giving water to the camels to show Abraham's servant which maiden to take home to wed Isaac. He has brought people together through chance meetings and similar schedules, social events and mutual friends. There is no limit on what God can do to accomplish His purpose and bring about His will.

To Evaluate

What does the statement above mean to you?

What situations do you face in which you need the Holy Spirit's guidance?

Is the Holy Spirit prompting you to get involved in something you have been hesitant about?

Is the Holy Spirit prompting you to stop your involvement in an activity or relationship?

Are you following the Holy Spirit's guidance in all areas of your life?

To Try

Claim a verse specifically about God's provision.

Find a song to encourage you that God is in control.

Pray about using matchmaking services. Follow the Holy Spirit's prompting in this area.

Read the book of Ruth.

Smile over something good every day

Go to bed smiling, resting in the Lord.

When the Slipper Finally Fits

Exactly two weeks after that lonely birthday, I got the call. "Remember that guy I told you about who works at the post office and wants to get married? Can I give him your number?" It was a dear friend from church on the other end of the line trying to help me meet a potential prince, but I was hesitant. What kind of guy randomly tells people that he wants to get married but doesn't even have a girlfriend? How desperate is he, and do I really want to get involved with him?

But then, my friend continued, "I've known his mother for years, and I've known him since he was little. He's a really great guy." She told me all about his family, how his mom grew up in Portugal, and how his dad was really laid back. She told me about his dark hair, pleasant demeanor, Christian character, and finally his name. Jeremy. Hmm. Then, she asked again, "Can I give him your number?" During the entire conversation, I had been praying about what I was supposed to do, asking God to show me if I should let her give him my phone number. In fact, I had prayed about it the day before when she had mentioned him at church. I was nervous about giving him my number and started saying so when a small voice inside said, "But what if he's the One?" So when she asked me this time, and I had peace from the Holy Spirit, I agreed.

As soon as I hung up with my friend, I ran upstairs. I felt so nervous and giddy that I was shaking. What she had told me

"

about this Jeremy made me hope that he would call, but what would I do if he did? Or didn't? What if he was really weird? What if he was awesome but didn't like me? What if I wasn't Cinderella but was actually the ugly stepsister, and the glass slipper was too small for my foot? I was scared. I stopped in the middle of my room and fell to my knees, praying that God would direct whatever was about to happen.

And then the phone rang.

Scripture

Sometimes we think that God isn't going to fulfill our dreams and desires, but He said, "If ye then, being evil, know how to give good gifts unto your children, how much more shall your Father which is in heaven give good things to them that ask him?" Matthew 7:11 (KJV).

When He finally does bring the desired answer to our prayers, how wonderful it is to be able to rejoice that we followed His plan during the waiting period! We read in Psalm 33:21, "For our heart shall rejoice in him, because we have trusted in his holy name (KJV)." We must continue trusting Him no matter how long the wait.

As we wait for the fulfillment of our deepest longings and after we receive the blessing of its satisfaction, we can praise God for His loving-kindness and for His place of refuge. The Bible says in Psalm 36:7, "How excellent is thy loving-kindness, O God! Therefore the children of men put their trust under the shadow of thy wings (KJV)."

Solution

The solution, this time, was definitely prayer. I had prayed about finding my prince on the internet but never joined a matchmaking site because I never had peace about doing so. I had been open to blind dates before but had never actually been set up on one. I had been rather wary of meeting this postal worker each time he had been mentioned, but no meeting had actually ever been arranged. Until now.

I answered the phone.

"Hello."

"Hi, my name is Jeremy. I'm calling for... Melinda... or Melissa—"

"This is *Melissa*." (No brownie points for him; he could've at least gotten my name right.)

"Oh yeah. A friend gave me your number and told me to call."

"Okay." (He was going to have to take the lead on this, or forget it!)

"So, I hear you've just moved back to Virginia?"

It wasn't the greatest opening line for a conversation, but it did get the ball rolling. Two-and-a-half hours later, when we finally hung up, I was glad I had been praying for God's guidance. Only He could've orchestrated such a meeting. This Jeremy guy did not want to hang up with me. Every time we reached a lull in the conversation, he asked, "What else can we talk about?" We exchanged testimonies, college stories, job plans, and life goals. We learned what things we had in common and where we differed in our opinions. He was funny and interesting and interested in me. The more we talked, the more compatible we seemed to be. Before we hung up, he asked how soon we could talk again. We set a time for the end of the week, but he called me after only three days. Twenty-three days and more than fifty hours of telephone conversations later, we finally met face to face.

Two months later, Jeremy proposed—on one knee with a gorgeous diamond ring balanced on top of a crystal glass slipper. The slipper couldn't actually be worn, but the ring fit perfectly. Eight months after that very first phone call, we met at the front of my hometown church and exchanged our vows in front of family and friends. Years of waiting, praying, wishing, and hoping for my prince charming to find me had finally come to an end. There I stood in my sparkling Cinderella wedding dress, "glass" slippers on my feet, and a glistening tiara on top of my head, pledging my love to this tall, dark, handsome man who could hardly wait to marry me.

Of all the ways I had dreamed about meeting my prince charming, I had never imagined an arranged telephone conversation followed a month later by an official first date. Yet, that was the plan God designed. His Holy Spirit prompted the miraculous workings of our fairy tale beginning and continued to guide us throughout the relationship. Our romance wasn't perfect, but it might not have happened at all if we hadn't been praying, seeking God's help with our longings and desires, trusting Him to show us the way, and following His leading wherever He chose. He brought us together. He helped us develop our relationship according to His guidelines laid out in the Bible, and He led us into the life we now have together. Because of Him, the glass slipper finally fit.

Something Extra...

To Think About

God has a unique plan for our lives. He plans trials to mold us into His likeness and blessings to show us His love. He knows the end from the beginning and everything in between. He leads us along the path He designs, desiring our love, our trust, and our praise along the way.

To Evaluate

What does the statement above mean to you?

How has God led you throughout your life so far?

What blessings has God given you for following His leading?

How have the trials He's brought you through drawn you closer to Him?

What situations have you faced that, when you look back on them, you can see God's Hand directing the circumstances?

To Try

Claim a verse specifically about God's love.

Find a song to remind you that God has a plan for you.

Write down the times that you have felt God's specific leading in your life. Read over it to remind yourself God cares what happens to you.

Write down ways that God has specifically blessed you. Remember when you read it that He will bless you, again, as you follow Him.

Pray daily for your future husband that God will protect him from all evil and bring him to you in His time.

Smile over something good every day.

Go to bed smiling, resting in the Lord.

Appendix: Running the Castle without a Prince

In spite of all my plans, I found myself facing new situations and new concerns as a single adult living alone. How do I handle a home and a job on my own? Is it acceptable to not clean the house if I'm the only one who lives there? To whom do I turn for advice, and whose authority am I under?

I offer the following thoughts, not as an exhaustive how-to list for living alone successfully but as a collection of considerations for single girls living away from their parents.

Establishing Your Home

If you're anything like me, you couldn't wait to get a home of your own so you could make it your own. After living in a dorm for six years, I felt so excited to finally be able to fill my apartment with all my own things—and only *my* things. I love looking around my apartment and seeing everything clean, neat, and put away. I come home and breathe a sigh of relief to be back in my sanctuary. For me, a clean house of my own is a beautiful thing.

Not everyone feels the same way, of course, but there are a few things we all should remember when living on our own.

1. If you want to make your house a home, have at it. If you desire to "nest" or make your house look a certain way, you don't have to wait until you're married to do so. Life doesn't

wait until you're married to begin, so why should you?

2. Maintain a clean house for yourself and for your future husband. Even if you could care less, clean your house. A clean house helps you maintain good health. Keeping it clean gives you good practice for married life—most men want their homes clean, even if they don't know how to clean it themselves. If you hate cleaning, hire a maid!

3. Establish a method for keeping your finances and bills in order. Whether you prefer a written budget or a computer record, find some way to keep your bills paid and your money accounted for. I know how much I can spend on food and such every month. I also have money put aside for emergencies—not a shopping emergency but a real emergency. I give myself an allowance to spend and put money into savings for the future. This way, if a need arises, I can handle it; when bills come, I can pay them; and when I do get married one day, I can help pay expenses or splurge on my honeymoon!

4. Be careful what habits you develop while you live alone. Do you do something now that your husband may find appalling? If so, could you stop if you needed to? Do you tell yourself, "I'll do it now, but I'll stop when I get married"? Remember that some habits can be very hard to break. Keep an eye on what you allow yourself to do, knowing what you believe your future to be.

Honoring Your Parents

For God commanded, saying, Honour thy father and mother: and, He that curseth father or mother, let him die the death.
Matthew 15:4 (KJV)

And he answered and said unto them, Have ye not read, that He which made them at the beginning made them male and female,

and said, For this cause shall a man leave father and mother, and shall cleave to his wife: and they twain shall be one flesh? Wherefore they are no more twain, but one flesh. What therefore God hath joined together, let not man put asunder.
Matthew 19:4-6 (KJV)

In the times of the Bible, young girls stayed at home until their fathers arranged for them to marry a man or to work for one. Girls had little or no say about whom they would marry, when they would marry, or where they would live before and after they married. But times change. Today, theoretically, we decide many of those things for ourselves, or at least have a say in them.

But while times and cultures change, the Bible remains constant. Its truths and principles apply no matter the day and age. With this in mind, how do we handle living alone?

1. We must remember that no matter how old we get or what our marital status is, we are always supposed to honor our parents. The Bible never says to honor your parents until you get married, as many may suppose. It simply tells us to honor them—apparently, forever.

2. We must recognize that until we marry, we are still under the authority of our parents. However, as we grow and mature, our parents may decide to relinquish that authority to us. It is our parents' authority, and it is their decision whether or not to pass that authority on to us. If you feel you have reached that age of maturity but your parents still exercise complete authority over you, you may wish to discuss it with them. Pray before you approach your parents, and realize that if you still live at home, it may be more difficult to come out from under their authority.

In my case, I moved one thousand miles away from my parents when I was twenty-four years old. I got my own job, made my own money, paid my own bills, and dealt with my own problems. I lived on my own. When I moved out, I did so with my parents' blessing and with their authority. They decided I was old enough and mature enough to make my own decisions, and they relinquished most of their authority over me to me. I still consult my parents and listen carefully to their advice, which is always freely offered, but they leave the decisions entirely in my hands. They have decided to let me decide.

Maintaining Your Testimony

As single women, there are certain aspects of maintaining a pure testimony that we must keep in mind as we live our lives from day to day. Until I lived alone, I never realized how much I needed to be aware not only of my actions but also of my surroundings and even my appearances. Here are a few areas to consider in maintaining your testimony.

1. You must be aware of where you go, what you do, who goes with you, and how you act while you're there. These things may seem rather obvious, but when you're single, you must be consciously aware of the image you're presenting— not because *image* is important but because your *testimony* is important. If you appear to flirt with all the guys, you'll probably get a reputation as a flirt, which may cause you to lose friends and have a hard time making new ones, let alone that special one. You may need to watch how much time you spend socializing with married or engaged men, even in public places, so as to not appear to be flirting with them. You must be careful to avoid meeting with men alone in a room where others cannot see what's happening inside. It boils down to protecting yourself from "scandal" as well as preventing temptation, which may strike even the most unlikely candidates. Thinking about your testimony and being aware of the picture you present is not always fun, but taking precautions is important not only to maintain your testimony but also to avoid temptation. And remember, keeping a good testimony is vital to maintaining a good

witness for Christ.

2. You must be careful when you go out alone. The basic idea of this point is to be aware of what's going on around you. These days, it's hardly safe to go to the store alone in broad daylight, let alone to shop in the twilight hours. I'm not saying we should be paranoid, but I am saying we should be prepared (keys ready to use, even as a weapon; cell phone handy or even in use; mace or pepper spray if it's legal to carry it), and we should be perceptive (watching who's around and where they're going; checking underneath and in the backseat of the car before entering it; keeping our eyes open and alert, always).

3. You must be careful whom you allow into your home and when. In other words, if you live alone, you should probably not have single guys over to your house. You should also be careful when repairmen come over. When a telephone repairman came to work on my phone lines, I had a friend over so that I would not be alone with a strange man in my apartment. Protect yourself and protect your testimony.

In order to maintain a pure testimony, you must be aware of the picture you present and how that picture may be interpreted. Some activities may be difficult to manage when you consider these things, but remember that the picture you present as a Christian ought to reflect the image of Christ.

Running a castle without a prince is no easy task, but you can do it —and do it well—until such time as your Prince Charming comes to help.

Acknowledgements

Catherine Wooten

Catherine Wooten is an amazingly talented artist who created all of the drawings included in this book. She also painted the beautiful glass slipper cover art. More of her original creations can be found here:

http://www.jcwootencell1.wixsite.com\drawingsbycat

William and Shelley Crawford

William (author, *Night of the Wolf*) and Shelley Crawford are my advisors, consultants, editors, supporters, and loving parents. Words cannot express enough my gratitude for them and for all they do for me.

My Family

From my siblings to my in-laws to my aunts and uncles and cousins, the support of our family has been a treasured blessing to me. Your faith in God shows in your lives and in the way we love and care for each other.

My Boys

We prayed for each of you before you were born, and we continue to pray for you as you grow. You bring joy and excitement to our home, and we love you. May you always follow God's leading and trust Him to bring you each your own beautiful Princess in His time.

My Charming Prince

Jeremy, you were worth the wait. I love living my life with you. Your humor keeps me smiling; your support is unmatched. You are the one my soul loves, always and forever.

<h1 style="text-align:center">About the Author</h1>

Melissa Gayle is a theatrical director and drama teacher who has degrees in writing and interpretive speech.   Her goal is to glorify God and point others to Him. After years of watching others find their fairytale ending, she finally met her charming prince. She is now living out her happily ever after with her husband and their four boys.

Photo credit: Sylvia Quiroz, Sylvia Quiroz Photos
Facebook, Instagram, Flickr

Night Of The Wolf

A Christian Fiction Adventure
by William Crawford and Melissa Gayle

Being beaten and kidnapped were not the activities wildlife biologist Jessica Baines had anticipated when she came to the popular Thunder Ridge ski resort to help Charlie Kimbrough, the local forest ranger, manage the havoc inflicted by an errant pack of wolves. How could she have known that what would confront her in the forest would not only threaten her life but also cause her to question everything she believed? What will she do? Will Charlie find her in time? Will either of them survive the Night of the Wolf?